VERSES

ON

LOVE

COMPILED BY Kyle Chambers
ALL VERSES ARE FROM THE KING JAMES BIBLE

LOVE

Deuteronomy 6:5 - And thou shalt love the LORD thy God with all thine heart, and with all thy soul, and with all thy might.

1 Corinthians 13:4-13 Charity suffereth long, [and] is kind; charity envieth not; charity vaunteth not itself, is not puffed up,

5 Doth not behave itself unseemly, seeketh not her own, is not easily provoked, thinketh no evil;

6 Rejoiceth not in iniquity, but rejoiceth in the truth;

7 Beareth all things, believeth all things, hopeth all things, endureth all things.

8 Charity never faileth: but whether [there be] prophecies, they shall fail; whether [there be] tongues, they shall cease; whether [there be] knowledge, it shall vanish away.

9 For we know in part, and we prophesy in part.

10 But when that which is perfect is come, then that which is in part shall be done away.

11 When I was a child, I spake as a child, I understood as a child, I thought as a child:

but when I became a man, I put away childish things.

12 For now we see through a glass, darkly; but then face to face: now I know in part; but then shall I know even as also I am known.

13 And now abideth faith, hope, charity, these three; but the greatest of these [is] charity.

Matthew 22:37-39 - 37 Jesus said unto him, Thou shalt love the Lord thy God with all thy heart, and with all thy soul, and with all thy mind.

38 This is the first and great commandment.

39 And the second [is] like unto it, Thou shalt love thy neighbour as thyself

1 Corinthians 16:14 - Let all your things be done with charity.

1 John 4:8 - He that loveth not knoweth not God; for God is love.

Leviticus 19:18 - Thou shalt not avenge, nor bear any grudge against the children of thy people, but thou shalt love thy neighbour as thyself: I [am] the LORD.

2 Chronicles 15:13 - That whosoever would not seek the LORD God of Israel should be put to

death, whether small or great, whether man or woman.

1 John 4:19 - We love him, because he first loved us.

1 John 4:12 - No man hath seen God at any time. If we love one another, God dwelleth in us, and his love is perfected in us.

1 John 4:18 - There is no fear in love; but perfect love casteth out fear: because fear hath torment. He that feareth is not made perfect in love.

Mark 12:30 - And thou shalt love the Lord thy God with all thy heart, and with all thy soul, and with all thy mind, and with all thy strength: this [is] the first commandment.

Galatians 5:22 - But the fruit of the Spirit is love, joy, peace, longsuffering, gentleness, goodness, faith,

1 Corinthians 13:13 - And now abideth faith, hope, charity, these three; but the greatest of these [is] charity.

John 14:15 - If ye love me, keep my commandments.

1 Corinthians 13:1-13 - [1] Though I speak with

the tongues of men and of angels, and have not charity, I am become [as] sounding brass, or a tinkling cymbal.

2 And though I have [the gift of] prophecy, and understand all mysteries, and all knowledge; and though I have all faith, so that I could remove mountains, and have not charity, I am nothing.

3 And though I bestow all my goods to feed [the poor], and though I give my body to be burned, and have not charity, it profiteth me nothing.

4 Charity suffereth long, [and] is kind; charity envieth not; charity vaunteth not itself, is not puffed up,

5 Doth not behave itself unseemly, seeketh not her own, is not easily provoked, thinketh no evil;

6 Rejoiceth not in iniquity, but rejoiceth in the truth;

7 Beareth all things, believeth all things, hopeth all things, endureth all things.

8 Charity never faileth: but whether [there be] prophecies, they shall fail; whether [there be] tongues, they shall cease; whether [there be] knowledge, it shall vanish away.

9 For we know in part, and we prophesy in part.

[10] But when that which is perfect is come, then that which is in part shall be done away.

[11] When I was a child, I spake as a child, I understood as a child, I thought as a child: but when I became a man, I put away childish things.

[12] For now we see through a glass, darkly; but then face to face: now I know in part; but then shall I know even as also I am known.

[13] And now abideth faith, hope, charity, these three; but the greatest of these [is] charity.

1 Timothy 1:5 - **Now the end of the commandment is charity out of a pure heart, and [of] a good conscience, and [of] faith unfeigned:**

1 Corinthians 13:8 - **Charity never faileth: but whether [there be] prophecies, they shall fail; whether [there be] tongues, they shall cease; whether [there be] knowledge, it shall vanish away.**

John 3:16 - **For God so loved the world, that he gave his only begotten Son, that whosoever believeth in him should not perish, but have everlasting life.**

1 Peter 4:8 - **And above all things have fervent charity among yourselves: for**

charity shall cover the multitude of sins.

Romans 8:38-39 [38] For I am persuaded, that neither death, nor life, nor angels, nor principalities, nor powers, nor things present, nor things to come,

[39] Nor height, nor depth, nor any other creature, shall be able to separate us from the love of God, which is in Christ Jesus our Lord.

1 Peter 2:17 - **Honour all [men]. Love the brotherhood. Fear God. Honour the king.**

1 John 4:7 - **Beloved, let us love one another: for love is of God; and every one that loveth is born of God, and knoweth God.**

Philippians 1:9 - **And this I pray, that your love may abound yet more and more in knowledge and [in] all judgment;**

Ephesians 4:32 - **And be ye kind one to another, tenderhearted, forgiving one another, even as God for Christ's sake hath forgiven you.**

Ephesians 6:24 - **Grace [be] with all them that love our Lord Jesus Christ in sincerity. Amen. ([To [the] Ephesians** written from Rome, by Tychicus.])

1 John 2:15 - **Love not the world, neither the things [that are] in the world. If any man love the world, the love of the Father is not in him.**

1 Thessalonians 5:11 - **Wherefore comfort yourselves together, and edify one another, even as also ye do.**

Matthew 22:37 - **Jesus said unto him, Thou shalt love the Lord thy God with all thy heart, and with all thy soul, and with all thy mind.**

Matthew 19:19 - **Honour thy father and [thy] mother: and, Thou shalt love thy neighbour as thyself.**

John 15:13 - **Greater love hath no man than this, that a man lay down his life for his friends.**

1 Timothy 6:10 - **For the love of money is the root of all evil: which while some coveted after, they have erred from the faith, and pierced themselves through with many sorrows.**

1 John 4:21 - **And this commandment have we from him, That he who loveth God love**

his brother also.

John 15:12 - **This is my commandment, That ye love one another, as I have loved you.**

1 Thessalonians 3:12 - **And the Lord make you to increase and abound in love one toward another, and toward all [men], even as we [do] toward you:**

1 John 3:18 - **My little children, let us not love in word, neither in tongue; but in deed and in truth.**

Revelation 3:19 - **As many as I love, I rebuke and chasten: be zealous therefore, and repent.**

2 Timothy 2:22 - **Flee also youthful lusts: but follow righteousness, faith, charity, peace, with them that call on the Lord out of a pure heart.**

Matthew 5:44-45 44 But I say unto you, Love your enemies, bless them that curse you, do good to them that hate you, and pray for them which despitefully use you, and persecute you;

45 That ye may be the children of your Father which is in heaven: for he maketh his sun to rise on the evil and on the good, and sendeth rain on the just and on the unjust.

1 Peter 3:9 - **Not rendering evil for evil, or railing for railing: but contrariwise blessing; knowing that ye are thereunto called, that ye should inherit a blessing.**

John 15:9-17 - [9] As the Father hath loved me, so have I loved you: continue ye in my love.

[10] If ye keep my commandments, ye shall abide in my love; even as I have kept my Father's commandments, and abide in his love.

[11] These things have I spoken unto you, that my joy might remain in you, and [that] your joy might be full.

[12] This is my commandment, That ye love one another, as I have loved you.

[13] Greater love hath no man than this, that a man lay down his life for his friends.

[14] Ye are my friends, if ye do whatsoever I command you.

[15] Henceforth I call you not servants; for the servant knoweth not what his lord doeth: but I have called you friends; for all things that I have heard of my Father I have made known unto you.

[16] Ye have not chosen me, but I have chosen you, and ordained you, that ye should go and bring forth fruit, and [that] your fruit should

remain: that whatsoever ye shall ask of the Father in my name, he may give it you.

[17] These things I command you, that ye love one another.

1 John 4:11 - **Beloved, if God so loved us, we ought also to love one another.**

1 Timothy 6:2 - **And they that have believing masters, let them not despise [them], because they are brethren; but rather do [them] service, because they are faithful and beloved, partakers of the benefit. These things teach and exhort.**

Matthew 25:34-40 [34] Then shall the King say unto them on his right hand, Come, ye blessed of my Father, inherit the kingdom prepared for you from the foundation of the world:

[35] For I was an hungred, and ye gave me meat: I was thirsty, and ye gave me drink: I was a stranger, and ye took me in:

[36] Naked, and ye clothed me: I was sick, and ye visited me: I was in prison, and ye came unto me.

[37] Then shall the righteous answer him, saying, Lord, when saw we thee an hungred, and fed [thee]? or thirsty, and gave [thee] drink?

³⁸ When saw we thee a stranger, and took [thee] in? or naked, and clothed [thee]?

³⁹ Or when saw we thee sick, or in prison, and came unto thee?

⁴⁰ And the King shall answer and say unto them, Verily I say unto you, Inasmuch as ye have done [it] unto one of the least of these my brethren, ye have done [it] unto me.

Matthew 10:42 - **And whosoever shall give to drink unto one of these little ones a cup of cold [water] only in the name of a disciple, verily I say unto you, he shall in no wise lose his reward.**

Mark 9:41 - **For whosoever shall give you a cup of water to drink in my name, because ye belong to Christ, verily I say unto you, he shall not lose his reward.**

Matthew 10:41 - **He that receiveth a prophet in the name of a prophet shall receive a prophet's reward; and he that receiveth a righteous man in the name of a righteous man shall receive a righteous man's reward.**

Galatians 5:14 - **For all the law is fulfilled in one word, [even] in this; Thou shalt love thy neighbour as thyself.**

Romans 13:8-10 - [8] Owe no man any thing, but to love one another: for he that loveth another hath fulfilled the law.

[9] For this, Thou shalt not commit adultery, Thou shalt not kill, Thou shalt not steal, Thou shalt not bear false witness, Thou shalt not covet; and if [there be] any other commandment, it is briefly comprehended in this saying, namely, Thou shalt love thy neighbour as thyself.

[10] Love worketh no ill to his neighbour: therefore love [is] the fulfilling of the law.

Mark 12:29-31 - [29] And Jesus answered him, The first of all the commandments [is], Hear, O Israel; The Lord our God is one Lord:

[30] And thou shalt love the Lord thy God with all thy heart, and with all thy soul, and with all thy mind, and with all thy strength: this [is] the first commandment.

[31] And the second [is] like, [namely] this, Thou shalt love thy neighbour as thyself. There is none other commandment greater than these.

Psalms 23:1-6 - ((A Psalm of David.) The LORD [is] my shepherd; I shall not want.

² He maketh me to lie down in green pastures: he leadeth me beside the still waters.

³ He restoreth my soul: he leadeth me in the paths of righteousness for his name's sake.

⁴ Yea, though I walk through the valley of the shadow of death, I will fear no evil: for thou [art] with me; thy rod and thy staff they comfort me.

⁵ Thou preparest a table before me in the presence of mine enemies: thou anointest my head with oil; my cup runneth over.

⁶ Surely goodness and mercy shall follow me all the days of my life: and I will dwell in the house of the LORD for ever

Romans 12:10 - [Be] kindly affectioned one to another with brotherly love; in honour preferring one another;

Ruth 1:16-17 - ¹⁶ And Ruth said, Intreat me not to leave thee, [or] to return from following after thee: for whither thou goest, I will go; and where thou lodgest, I will lodge: thy people [shall be] my people, and thy God my God:

¹⁷ Where thou diest, will I die, and there will I be buried: the LORD do so to me, and more also, [if ought] but death part thee and me.

Philippians 2:2 - **Fulfil ye my joy, that ye be likeminded, having the same love, [being] of one accord, of one mind.**

Galatians 5:26 - **Let us not be desirous of vain glory, provoking one another, envying one another.**

Galatians 5:22-23 - 22 But the fruit of the Spirit is love, joy, peace, longsuffering, gentleness, goodness, faith,

23 Meekness, temperance: against such there is no law.

Mark 12:31 - **And the second [is] like, [namely] this, Thou shalt love thy neighbour as thyself. There is none other commandment greater than these.**

Psalms 27:7 - **Hear, O LORD, [when] I cry with my voice: have mercy also upon me, and answer me.**

1 John 5:2 - **By this we know that we love the children of God, when we love God, and keep his commandments.**

1 John 2:9-11 9 He that saith he is in the light, and hateth his brother, is in darkness even until now.

¹⁰ He that loveth his brother abideth in the light, and there is none occasion of stumbling in him.

¹¹ But he that hateth his brother is in darkness, and walketh in darkness, and knoweth not whither he goeth, because that darkness hath blinded his eyes.

Galatians 6:10 **- As we have therefore opportunity, let us do good unto all [men], especially unto them who are of the household of faith.**

Romans 14:19 **- Let us therefore follow after the things which make for peace, and things wherewith one may edify another.**

Ephesians 3:17-19 ¹⁷ That Christ may dwell in your hearts by faith; that ye, being rooted and grounded in love,

¹⁸ May be able to comprehend with all saints what [is] the breadth, and length, and depth, and height;

¹⁹ And to know the love of Christ, which passeth knowledge, that ye might be filled with all the fulness of God.

Romans 15:7 **- Wherefore receive ye one another, as Christ also received us to the glory of God.**

John 15:17 - These things I command you, that ye love one another.

Luke 10:1-27 [1] After these things the Lord appointed other seventy also, and sent them two and two before his face into every city and place, whither he himself would come.

[2] Therefore said he unto them, The harvest truly [is] great, but the labourers [are] few: pray ye therefore the Lord of the harvest, that he would send forth labourers into his harvest.

[3] Go your ways: behold, I send you forth as lambs among wolves.

[4] Carry neither purse, nor scrip, nor shoes: and salute no man by the way.

[5] And into whatsoever house ye enter, first say, Peace [be] to this house.

[6] And if the son of peace be there, your peace shall rest upon it: if not, it shall turn to you again.

[7] And in the same house remain, eating and drinking such things as they give: for the labourer is worthy of his hire. Go not from house to house.

[8] And into whatsoever city ye enter, and they receive you, eat such things as are set before you:

⁹ And heal the sick that are therein, and say unto them, The kingdom of God is come nigh unto you.

¹⁰ But into whatsoever city ye enter, and they receive you not, go your ways out into the streets of the same, and say,

¹¹ Even the very dust of your city, which cleaveth on us, we do wipe off against you: notwithstanding be ye sure of this, that the kingdom of God is come nigh unto you.

¹² But I say unto you, that it shall be more tolerable in that day for Sodom, than for that city.

¹³ Woe unto thee, Chorazin! woe unto thee, Bethsaida! for if the mighty works had been done in Tyre and Sidon, which have been done in you, they had a great while ago repented, sitting in sackcloth and ashes.

¹⁴ But it shall be more tolerable for Tyre and Sidon at the judgment, than for you.

¹⁵ And thou, Capernaum, which art exalted to heaven, shalt be thrust down to hell.

¹⁶ He that heareth you heareth me; and he that despiseth you despiseth me; and he that despiseth me despiseth him that sent me.

¹⁷ And the seventy returned again with joy, saying, Lord, even the devils are subject unto us through thy name.

[18] And he said unto them, I beheld Satan as lightning fall from heaven.

[19] Behold, I give unto you power to tread on serpents and scorpions, and over all the power of the enemy: and nothing shall by any means hurt you.

[20] Notwithstanding in this rejoice not, that the spirits are subject unto you; but rather rejoice, because your names are written in heaven.

[21] In that hour Jesus rejoiced in spirit, and said, I thank thee, O Father, Lord of heaven and earth, that thou hast hid these things from the wise and prudent, and hast revealed them unto babes: even so, Father; for so it seemed good in thy sight.

[22] All things are delivered to me of my Father: and no man knoweth who the Son is, but the Father; and who the Father is, but the Son, and [he] to whom the Son will reveal [him].

[23] And he turned him unto [his] disciples, and said privately, Blessed [are] the eyes which see the things that ye see:

[24] For I tell you, that many prophets and kings have desired to see those things which ye see, and have not seen [them]; and to hear those things which ye hear, and have not heard [them].

[25] And, behold, a certain lawyer stood up, and tempted him, saying, Master, what shall I do to inherit eternal life?

[26] He said unto him, What is written in the law? how readest thou?

[27] And he answering said, Thou shalt love the Lord thy God with all thy heart, and with all thy soul, and with all thy strength, and with all thy mind; and thy neighbour as thyself.

Song of Solomon 8:6-7 - [6] Set me as a seal upon thine heart, as a seal upon thine arm: for love [is] strong as death; jealousy [is] cruel as the grave: the coals thereof [are] coals of fire, [which hath a] most vehement flame.

[7] Many waters cannot quench love, neither can the floods drown it: if [a] man would give all the substance of his house for love, it would utterly be contemned.

1 John 3:11 - For this is the message that ye heard from the beginning, that we should love one another.

1 John 2:5 - But whoso keepeth his word, in him verily is the love of God perfected: hereby know we that we are in him.

1 Peter 1:8 - **Whom having not seen, ye love; in whom, though now ye see [him] not, yet believing, ye rejoice with joy unspeakable and full of glory:**

Galatians 4:20 - **I desire to be present with you now, and to change my voice; for I stand in doubt of you.**

1 Corinthians 13:4 - **Charity suffereth long, [and] is kind; charity envieth not; charity vaunteth not itself, is not puffed up,**

John 13:34 - **A new commandment I give unto you, That ye love one another; as I have loved you, that ye also love one another.**

Isaiah 1:1-31 - [1] The vision of Isaiah the son of Amoz, which he saw concerning Judah and Jerusalem in the days of Uzziah, Jotham, Ahaz, [and] Hezekiah, kings of Judah.

[2] Hear, O heavens, and give ear, O earth: for the LORD hath spoken, I have nourished and brought up children, and they have rebelled against me.

[3] The ox knoweth his owner, and the ass his master's crib: [but] Israel doth not know, my people doth not consider.

[4] Ah sinful nation, a people laden with iniquity, a seed of evildoers, children that are

corrupters: they have forsaken the LORD, they have provoked the Holy One of Israel unto anger, they are gone away backward.

5 Why should ye be stricken any more? ye will revolt more and more: the whole head is sick, and the whole heart faint.

6 From the sole of the foot even unto the head [there is] no soundness in it; [but] wounds, and bruises, and putrifying sores: they have not been closed, neither bound up, neither mollified with ointment.

7 Your country [is] desolate, your cities [are] burned with fire: your land, strangers devour it in your presence, and [it is] desolate, as overthrown by strangers.

8 And the daughter of Zion is left as a cottage in a vineyard, as a lodge in a garden of cucumbers, as a besieged city.

9 Except the LORD of hosts had left unto us a very small remnant, we should have been as Sodom, [and] we should have been like unto Gomorrah.

10 Hear the word of the LORD, ye rulers of Sodom; give ear unto the law of our God, ye people of Gomorrah.

11 To what purpose [is] the multitude of your sacrifices unto me? saith the LORD: I am full of the burnt offerings of rams, and the fat of

fed beasts; and I delight not in the blood of bullocks, or of lambs, or of he goats.

12 When ye come to appear before me, who hath required this at your hand, to tread my courts?

13 Bring no more vain oblations; incense is an abomination unto me; the new moons and sabbaths, the calling of assemblies, I cannot away with; [it is] iniquity, even the solemn meeting.

14 Your new moons and your appointed feasts my soul hateth: they are a trouble unto me; I am weary to bear [them].

15 And when ye spread forth your hands, I will hide mine eyes from you: yea, when ye make many prayers, I will not hear: your hands are full of blood.

16 Wash you, make you clean; put away the evil of your doings from before mine eyes; cease to do evil;

17 Learn to do well; seek judgment, relieve the oppressed, judge the fatherless, plead for the widow.

18 Come now, and let us reason together, saith the LORD: though your sins be as scarlet, they shall be as white as snow; though they be red like crimson, they shall be as wool.

¹⁹ If ye be willing and obedient, ye shall eat the good of the land:

²⁰ But if ye refuse and rebel, ye shall be devoured with the sword: for the mouth of the LORD hath spoken [it].

²¹ How is the faithful city become an harlot! it was full of judgment; righteousness lodged in it; but now murderers.

²² Thy silver is become dross, thy wine mixed with water:

²³ Thy princes [are] rebellious, and companions of thieves: every one loveth gifts, and followeth after rewards: they judge not the fatherless, neither doth the cause of the widow come unto them.

²⁴ Therefore saith the Lord, the LORD of hosts, the mighty One of Israel, Ah, I will ease me of mine adversaries, and avenge me of mine enemies:

²⁵ And I will turn my hand upon thee, and purely purge away thy dross, and take away all thy tin:

²⁶ And I will restore thy judges as at the first, and thy counsellors as at the beginning: afterward thou shalt be called, The city of righteousness, the faithful city.

²⁷ Zion shall be redeemed with judgment, and her converts with righteousness.

²⁸ And the destruction of the transgressors and of the sinners [shall be] together, and they that forsake the LORD shall be consumed.

²⁹ For they shall be ashamed of the oaks which ye have desired, and ye shall be confounded for the gardens that ye have chosen.

³⁰ For ye shall be as an oak whose leaf fadeth, and as a garden that hath no water.

³¹ And the strong shall be as tow, and the maker of it as a spark, and they shall both burn together, and none shall quench [them].

Jude 1:21 - **Keep yourselves in the love of God, looking for the mercy of our Lord Jesus Christ unto eternal life.**

1 John 5:3 - **For this is the love of God, that we keep his commandments: and his commandments are not grievous.**

1 John 4:7-16 - ⁷ Beloved, let us love one another: for love is of God; and every one that loveth is born of God, and knoweth God.

⁸ He that loveth not knoweth not God; for God is love.

⁹ In this was manifested the love of God toward us, because that God sent his only begotten Son into the world, that we might live through him.

[10] Herein is love, not that we loved God, but that he loved us, and sent his Son [to be] the propitiation for our sins.

[11] Beloved, if God so loved us, we ought also to love one another.

[12] No man hath seen God at any time. If we love one another, God dwelleth in us, and his love is perfected in us.

[13] Hereby know we that we dwell in him, and he in us, because he hath given us of his Spirit.

[14] And we have seen and do testify that the Father sent the Son [to be] the Saviour of the world.

[15] Whosoever shall confess that Jesus is the Son of God, God dwelleth in him, and he in God.

[16] And we have known and believed the love that God hath to us. God is love; and he that dwelleth in love dwelleth in God, and God in him.

1 John 3:23 - And this is his commandment, That we should believe on the name of his Son Jesus Christ, and love one another, as he gave us commandment.

1 John 3:17 - **But whoso hath this world's good, and seeth his brother have need, and shutteth up his bowels [of compassion] from him, how dwelleth the love of God in him?**

1 John 3:16-19 [16] Hereby perceive we the love [of God], because he laid down his life for us: and we ought to lay down [our] lives for the brethren.

[17] But whoso hath this world's good, and seeth his brother have need, and shutteth up his bowels [of compassion] from him, how dwelleth the love of God in him?

[18] My little children, let us not love in word, neither in tongue; but in deed and in truth.

[19] And hereby we know that we are of the truth, and shall assure our hearts before him.

John 3:16 - 3:17[16] For God so loved the world, that he gave his only begotten Son, that whosoever believeth in him should not perish, but have everlasting life.

[17] For God sent not his Son into the world to condemn the world; but that the world through him might be saved.

1 Peter 3:8 - **Finally, [be ye] all of one**

mind, having compassion one of another, love as brethren, [be] pitiful, [be] courteous:

Hebrews 6:10 - **For God [is] not unrighteous to forget your work and labour of love, which ye have shewed toward his name, in that ye have ministered to the saints, and do minister.**

2 Timothy 1:4 - **Greatly desiring to see thee, being mindful of thy tears, that I may be filled with joy;**

Colossians 2:1 - **For I would that ye knew what great conflict I have for you, and [for] them at Laodicea, and [for] as many as have not seen my face in the flesh;**

1 Corinthians 13:4-8 ⁴ Charity suffereth long, [and] is kind; charity envieth not; charity vaunteth not itself, is not puffed up,

⁵ Doth not behave itself unseemly, seeketh not her own, is not easily provoked, thinketh no evil;

⁶ Rejoiceth not in iniquity, but rejoiceth in the truth;

⁷ Beareth all things, believeth all things, hopeth all things, endureth all things.

[8] Charity never faileth: but whether [there be] prophecies, they shall fail; whether [there be] tongues, they shall cease; whether [there be] knowledge, it shall vanish away.

Luke 10:27-30 - [27] And he answering said, Thou shalt love the Lord thy God with all thy heart, and with all thy soul, and with all thy strength, and with all thy mind; and thy neighbour as thyself.

[28] And he said unto him, Thou hast answered right: this do, and thou shalt live.

[29] But he, willing to justify himself, said unto Jesus, And who is my neighbour?

[30] And Jesus answering said, A certain [man] went down from Jerusalem to Jericho, and fell among thieves, which stripped him of his raiment, and wounded [him], and departed, leaving [him] half dead.

Matthew 5:3-10 [3] Blessed [are] the poor in spirit: for theirs is the kingdom of heaven.

[4] Blessed [are] they that mourn: for they shall be comforted.

[5] Blessed [are] the meek: for they shall inherit the earth.

[6] Blessed [are] they which do hunger and thirst after righteousness: for they shall be filled.

[7] Blessed [are] the merciful: for they shall obtain mercy.

[8] Blessed [are] the pure in heart: for they shall see God.

[9] Blessed [are] the peacemakers: for they shall be called the children of God.

[10] Blessed [are] they which are persecuted for righteousness' sake: for theirs is the kingdom of heaven.

Psalms 127:1-26 - [1] (A Song of degrees for Solomon.) Except the LORD build the house, they labour in vain that build it: except the LORD keep the city, the watchman waketh [but] in vain.

[2] [It is] vain for you to rise up early, to sit up late, to eat the bread of sorrows: [for] so he giveth his beloved sleep.

[3] Lo, children [are] an heritage of the LORD: [and] the fruit of the womb [is his] reward.

[4] As arrows [are] in the hand of a mighty man; so [are] children of the youth.

[5] Happy [is] the man that hath his quiver full of them: they shall not be ashamed, but they shall speak with the enemies in the gate.

Psalms 1:1-6 [1] Blessed [is] the man that walketh not in the counsel of the ungodly, nor standeth in the way of sinners, nor sitteth in the seat of the scornful.

[2] But his delight [is] in the law of the LORD; and in his law doth he meditate day and night.

[3] And he shall be like a tree planted by the rivers of water, that bringeth forth his fruit in his season; his leaf also shall not wither; and whatsoever he doeth shall prosper.

[4] The ungodly [are] not so: but [are] like the chaff which the wind driveth away.

[5] Therefore the ungodly shall not stand in the judgment, nor sinners in the congregation of the righteous.

[6] For the LORD knoweth the way of the righteous: but the way of the ungodly shall perish.

Joshua 1:9 - Have not I commanded thee? Be strong and of a good courage; be not afraid, neither be thou dismayed: for the LORD thy God [is] with thee whithersoever thou goest.

Revelation 2:4 - Nevertheless I have [somewhat] against thee, because thou hast left thy first love.

2 John 1:6 - And this is love, that we walk after his commandments. This is the commandment, That, as ye have heard from the beginning, ye should walk in it.

1 John 5:1 - Whosoever believeth that Jesus is the Christ is born of God: and every one that loveth him that begat loveth him also that is begotten of him.

1 John 3:14 - We know that we have passed from death unto life, because we love the brethren. He that loveth not [his] brother abideth in death.

James 2:8 - If ye fulfil the royal law according to the scripture, Thou shalt love thy neighbour as thyself, ye do well:

James 1:27 - Pure religion and undefiled before God and the Father is this, To visit the fatherless and widows in their affliction, [and] to keep himself unspotted from the world.

James 1:12 - Blessed [is] the man that endureth temptation: for when he is tried, he shall receive the crown of life, which the Lord hath promised to them that love him.

Hebrews 10:24 - And let us consider one another to provoke unto love and to good works:

Printed in Great Britain
by Amazon